P9-BJV-441

Fact Finders®

GENETICS

PLANT CELLS

by Mason Anders

CAPSTONE PRESS
a capstone imprint

Fact Finders Books are published by Capstone Press,
1710 Roe Crest Drive, North Mankato, Minnesota 56003
www.mycapstone.com

Library of Congress Cataloging-in-Publication Data
Names: Anders, Mason, author.
Title: Plant cells / by Mason Anders.
Description: North Mankato, Minnesota : Capstone Press, [2017] | Series: Fact finders. Genetics |
   Audience: Ages 8–10. | Audience: Grades 4 to 6. | Includes bibliographical references and index.
Identifiers: LCCN 2016055785
   ISBN 978-1-5157-7258-3 (library binding)
   ISBN 978-1-5157-7262-0 (paperback)|
   ISBN 978-1-5157-7266-8 (ebook pdf)
Subjects: LCSH: Plant cells and tissues—Juvenile literature.
Classification: LCC QK725 .A537 2017 | DDC 581.7—dc23
LC record available at https://lccn.loc.gov/2016055785

Editorial Credits
Editor: Nikki Potts
Designer: Philippa Jenkins
Media Researcher: Morgan Walters and Jo Miller
Production Specialist: Katy LaVigne

Photo Credits
iStockphoto: NNehring, cover, (bottom), 3; Capstone: Oxford Designers & Illustrators, 18; Science Source: Benjamin Campillo, 12; Shutterstock: Alila Medical Media, 23 (bottom), Aranami, 11, AustralianCamera, 21, BlueRingMedia, 8, 10 (both), 14, Designua, 28, Dimarion, 15, ellepigrafica, 20, Elliotte Rusty Harold, 23 (top), Gilmanshin, 5, gritsalak karalak, 25, JP Chretien, 4, Kazakova Maryia, 24, Mopic, 19, NoPainNoGain, 7, Petr Baumann, 26, PIYAPONG THONGDUMHYU, 1, sciencepics, 22, special for you, throughout, (background), Tarica, cover (top), toeytoey, 6, udaix, 13, Wire_man, 16

Printed and bound in China.
004640

TABLE OF CONTENTS

CHAPTER 1

What Is a Plant Cell?

The thick branches of an oak tree. A beautiful rose. Tall prairie grasses. Soft moss on a forest floor. Trees, flowers, grasses, and moss are all different kinds of plants. Our planet hosts more than 260,000 species of plants that come in an astonishing variety.

Meadows alone can have hundreds of different flower, grass, and other plant species.

From roots to leaves, every plant is made of millions of cells.

No matter how they vary, every single plant is made of a basic building block — a cell. A cell is the smallest unit of life. It provides the basic structure and function for plants and every other living thing. Most cells are so tiny it takes a microscope to see them. The bigger the plant, the more cells it has. A single maple tree has trillions of cells.

Each cell is a self-contained unit. A plant cell is constantly working. It makes food, and it releases energy from food to power different life processes. It gives off waste products, such as water vapor and oxygen. Plant cells are constantly dividing to grow deeper roots, taller stems, or new buds, seeds, and fruit.

Each plant cell has its own job. For example, special cells in the stem carry water up from the roots. Green cells in the leaves make food. How cells are arranged and what jobs they do create the differences from plant to plant.

microscopic plant cells

Plant cells form the basis of life on Earth. Cells of green plants, unlike animal cells, make their own food using energy from sunlight. Plants trap the sun's energy, which becomes the basis of food chains. Some animals eat plants for food. Other animals eat plant-eating animals. The energy from the sun used by plants to make food is passed along from plant cells to animal cells.

As plants make their own food, they also give off oxygen. Both plants and animals need oxygen to live. By forming the basis of food chains and making oxygen, plant cells make life on Earth possible.

FACT

In the food chain, plants are known as primary producers. They are the primary source of all food on Earth.

All food chains begin with plants and end with decomposers. Decomposers break down the remains of dead plants and animals. They release nutrients back into the ground. These nutrients are necessary for plants.

Two Borders

A plant cell is enclosed by two borders: a cell wall and a cell membrane.

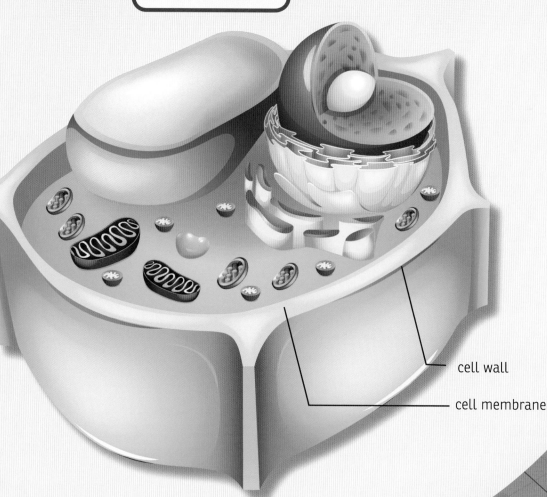

Plant Cell

cell wall

cell membrane

Cell Wall

A plant cell is surrounded by a boxy cell wall. Compared to other cell parts, cell walls are thick and strong. Cell walls protect plant cells and make them sturdy. They allow plants to grow tall without any bones to hold them up.

Cell walls have openings connecting one cell to another. These allow water, food, and nutrients to flow freely throughout the plant. Water can also escape through these holes. This is what happens when a plant **wilts**. But even as the cell shrivels up, the cell wall holds its basic shape. When the plant is watered, it will stand tall again.

About one-third of all plant matter is **cellulose**. This is the material that makes up most cell walls. Plants make cellulose from sugar. But unlike simple sugar, tough cellulose cannot be dissolved in water. Cellulose fibers give wood its strength. They make up most of the cotton, paper, and other plant products we use.

Cell Membrane

Imagine the cell wall is like a box. The cell membrane is like a balloon inside it. This soft, stretchy skin holds the cell together. It also acts as the cell's security system. It monitors what passes in and out of the cell. A cell membrane's tiny holes let in only what the plant cell needs to live, such as water and nutrients. It lets out only wastes and other chemicals the cell does not need.

wilt—to droop

cellulose—material that helps make cell walls stiff and rigid

CHAPTER 3

The Nucleus

The nucleus is the control center of a plant cell. It works like the brain does in humans. It gives directions to the rest of the cell. The nucleus directs the cell through two important molecules — DNA and RNA.

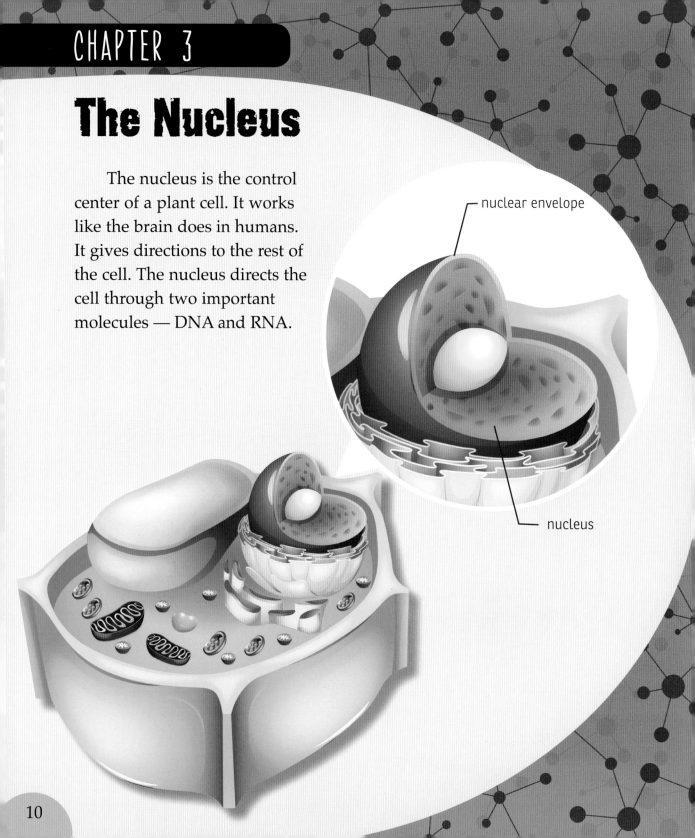

nuclear envelope

nucleus

DNA

The nucleus encloses and protects deoxyribonucleic acid, or DNA. All the activities that a cell carries out depend on the DNA molecule. DNA is made up of groups of chemicals arranged in patterns. These patterns make up a code.

A plant's DNA code provides instructions about how a cell should build and maintain a plant. A single unit of this code is called a **gene**. Each gene codes for something different. For example, a gene may determine the color of a flower or the texture of bark. Genes direct what species a plant will be, whether it makes cones or fruit, if it has broad leaves or needles, and thousands of other **traits**. Genes also determine how many seeds a plant makes. Cells in seeds carry DNA to pass on to another generation of plants.

BASES

The chemicals that make up DNA are known as bases. They are adenine (A), thymine (T), cytosine (C), and guanine (G). Adenine joins with thymine, and cytosine joins with guanine. Each bond forms a rung in the twisted ladder structure of a DNA strand. Cells read base patterns three-letter words, or codons, at a time. Each codon means something different. For example, "TGA" means stop.

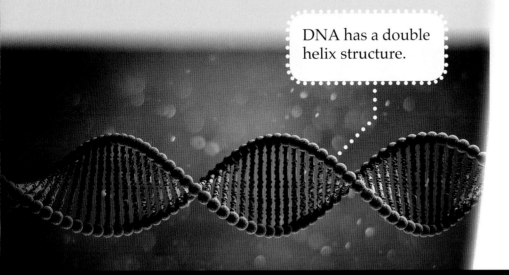

DNA has a double helix structure.

gene—tiny unit of a cell that determines the characteristics that an offspring gets from his or her parents

trait—a quality or characteristic that makes one person or animal different from another

RNA

The nuclear envelope surrounds and protects the nucleus. Some substances can flow in and out through tiny pores in the membrane. However, DNA never leaves the nucleus — it is too important. Instead, the information in DNA is copied onto another molecule called ribonucleic acid, or RNA. RNA is like a messenger. It can leave the nucleus. RNA carries DNA's instructions to the rest of the cell.

RNA carries genetic information from DNA inside the nucleus to **ribosomes** outside the nucleus.

ribosome—structure that helps put together proteins

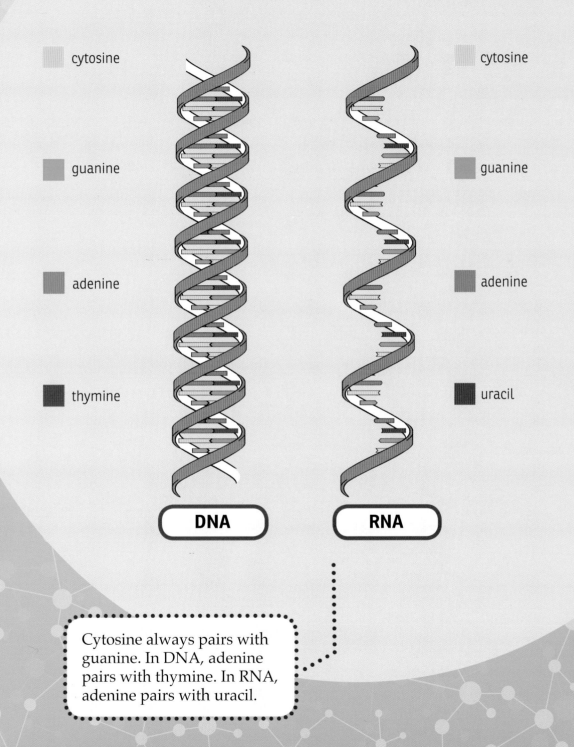

cytosine

guanine

adenine

thymine

cytosine

guanine

adenine

uracil

DNA

RNA

Cytosine always pairs with guanine. In DNA, adenine pairs with thymine. In RNA, adenine pairs with uracil.

CHAPTER 4

Organelles

Surrounding the nucleus is a region called the cytoplasm. Here, **organelles** perform the cell's jobs. These include making and sorting molecules, removing waste, and storing food and water. A plant cell has three main organelles. These are the central vacuole, chloroplasts, and mitochondria.

FACT

Along with the cell wall, the central vacuole helps hold the plant up. It fills with water and presses outward to give the cell wall strength.

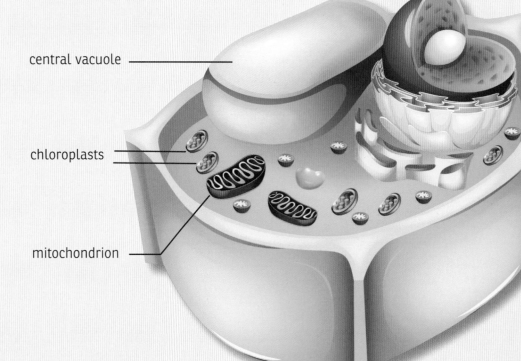

central vacuole

chloroplasts

mitochondrion

organelle—a small structure in a cell that performs a specific function and is surrounded by its own membrane

Central Vacuole

Looking at a plant cell through a microscope, you will usually see one structure that is quite a bit larger than the others. Most likely, this is the cell's central vacuole. This large pouch stores food and water for the plant. Chemical waste goes here too, where it mixes with water. When a plant lets water vapor out through its pores, waste leaves the plant as well.

Chloroplasts

Some plant cells have up to 100 small green organelles in their cytoplasm. These are called chloroplasts. Their job is to make food through the process of **photosynthesis**.

Chloroplasts contain chlorophyll, a green substance that captures energy from sunlight. It then changes that energy into a form the plant can use. In addition to sunlight, photosynthesis requires water and carbon dioxide gas from the air. Using these three ingredients — sunlight, water, and carbon dioxide — chloroplasts make simple sugar molecules called glucose and give off oxygen.

Chlorophyll gives plant cells their green color.

photosynthesis—the process by which plants make food using sunlight, carbon dioxide, and water

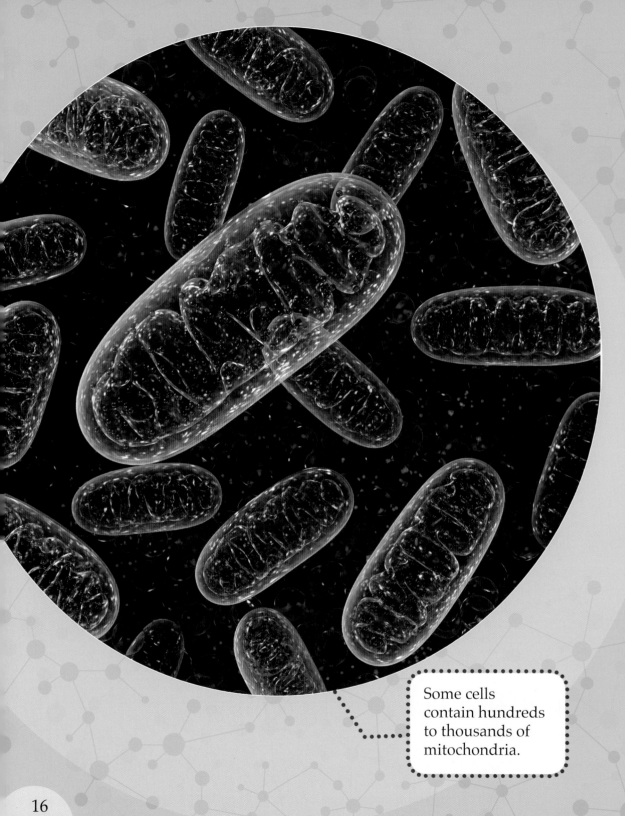

Some cells contain hundreds to thousands of mitochondria.

Mitochondria

Mitochondria are the power plants of the cell. They provide the energy a plant cell needs to do all of its jobs. Like power plants, mitochondria need fuel to work. In green plants, mitochondria get their fuel from the glucose made during photosynthesis.

A glucose molecule holds plenty of food energy, but a plant cell cannot use it directly. The glucose must first be **converted**. Mitochondria convert the glucose into a chemical called adenosine triphosphate, or ATP. The cell uses ATP to power just about every job, such as making molecules and moving them to where they need to go.

This process of converting glucose to ATP is called **cellular respiration**. Because it requires oxygen, most people think of cellular respiration in terms of breathing in animals. However, plants also rely on this crucial life process. Plants use oxygen just like we do. However, they make even more oxygen than they can use. And it's a good thing too! This leftover oxygen goes into the atmosphere to be used by animals and people.

convert—to turn something into something else

cellular respiration—process used by cells to break down food molecules into small units of energy

CHAPTER 5

Photosynthesis and Cellular Respiration

A terrarium is an enclosed, see-through habitat for plants. No air gets in or out, and yet a plant can live inside it for weeks or longer. How can that be? The answer has to do with the ingredients and **by-products** of both photosynthesis and cellular respiration.

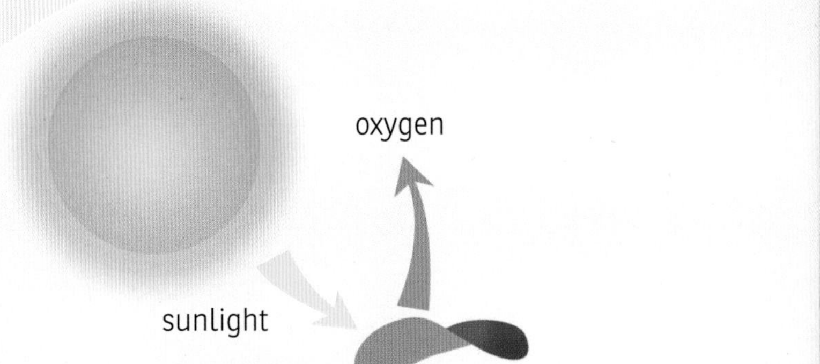

During photosynthesis plants take carbon dioxide out of the air and release oxygen back into it.

oxygen

sunlight

carbon dioxide

water

by-product—something that is left over after you make or do something

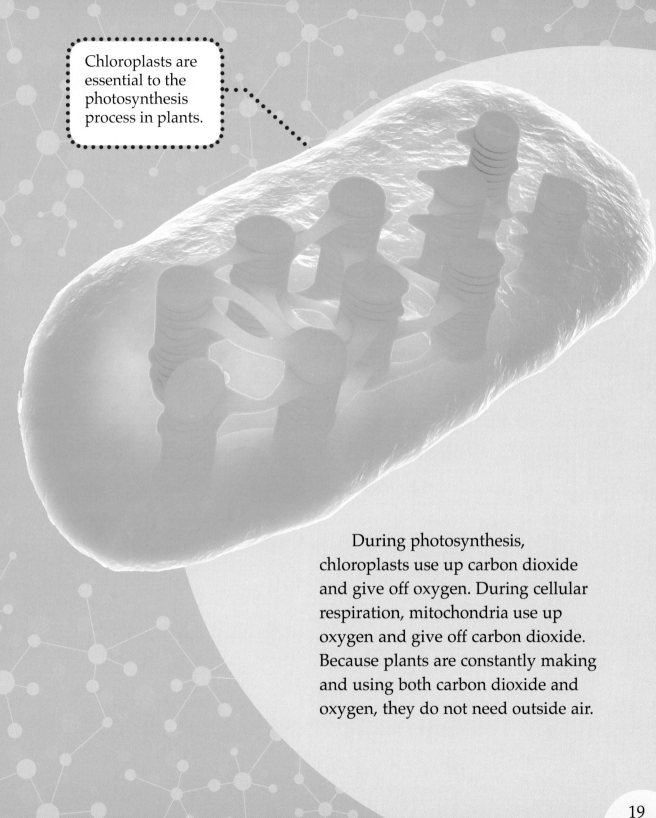

Chloroplasts are essential to the photosynthesis process in plants.

During photosynthesis, chloroplasts use up carbon dioxide and give off oxygen. During cellular respiration, mitochondria use up oxygen and give off carbon dioxide. Because plants are constantly making and using both carbon dioxide and oxygen, they do not need outside air.

Photosynthesis and cellular respiration can be thought of as opposite processes. In photosynthesis, sunlight, water, and carbon dioxide make glucose and oxygen. In turn, these two by-products — glucose and oxygen — form the ingredients for cellular respiration. In the mitochondria, they react to create ATP.

As shown in the diagram below, glucose molecules start the first phase of cellular respiration called glycolysis. During this phase, glucose is broken down into pyruvate molecules. These molecules then enter the mitochondrion. One carbon dioxide and one hydrogen molecule from each pyruvate produce an **acetyl group** and join with a CoA enzyme.

The acetyl CoA then forms a carbon compound during the Krebs cycle — phase two. Two ATP molecules are produced during this phase. Next is the electron transport chain. During this phase, **oxidation** of glucose occurs. Each glucose molecule leads to the production of about 32 to 34 ATP molecules. As ATP is created, carbon dioxide is released. This carbon dioxide can then be used for photosynthesis, which gives off more oxygen. And so, the two processes fuel each other.

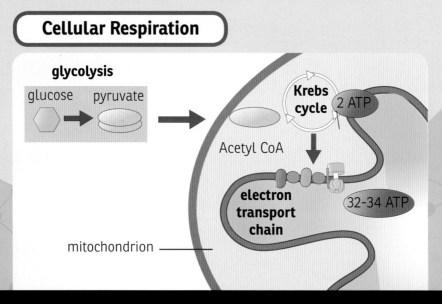

Cellular Respiration

glycolysis

glucose → pyruvate

Krebs cycle — 2 ATP

Acetyl CoA

electron transport chain — 32-34 ATP

mitochondrion

acetyl group—a group of acetic acid

oxidation—the act or process of combining with oxygen

THE IMPORTANCE OF PLANTS AND TREES

Plants and trees greatly contribute to our environment by releasing oxygen and taking in carbon dioxide during photosynthesis. According to the U.S. Department of Agriculture, "One acre of forest absorbs six tons of carbon dioxide and puts out four tons of oxygen. This is enough to meet the annual needs of 18 people." Plants also help filter the air. They absorb other pollutants such as carbon monoxide.

CHAPTER 6

Cell Division and Plant Growth

Plants cells divide two ways: meiosis and mitosis. Meiosis produces gametes, egg and sperm cells, which are needed for reproduction. For most plants, reproduction begins in flowers. Dusty yellow **pollen** carries sperm cells. At the base of the flower, the ovary holds egg cells. When a sperm cell unites with an egg's nucleus, an embryo forms. The embryo contains a single cell with DNA from the sperm and egg.

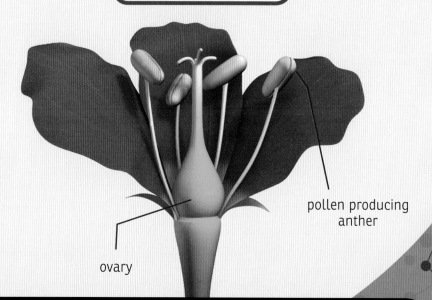

Parts of a Flower

pollen producing anther

ovary

pollen—a powder made by flowers containing sperm produced by a plant's male organs

Bees transfer pollen from one flower to another, allowing reproduction to begin.

MEIOSIS II

Meiosis happens in two stages — meiosis I and meiosis II. Each stage has four main phases: prophase, metaphase, anaphase, and telophase. During meiosis II, four gametes are produced. Each contains half of the DNA from one parent cell.

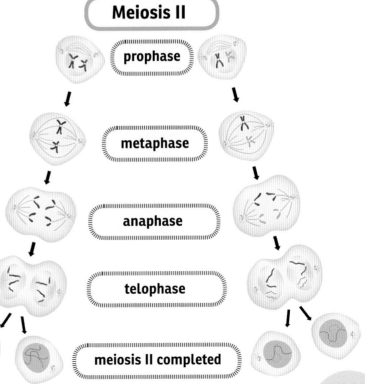

Meiosis II

prophase

metaphase

anaphase

telophase

meiosis II completed

Cell Division and Plant Life Cycles

Cell reproduction uses a lot of energy. Plants need plenty of food to support the growth of new cells. For this reason, young plants put most of their energy into producing leaves. Flowers, fruit, and seeds appear only when a plant is big enough to produce the food — and energy — needed to reproduce.

Stages in an apple tree's life cycle include a seed, sprout, sapling, and mature tree.

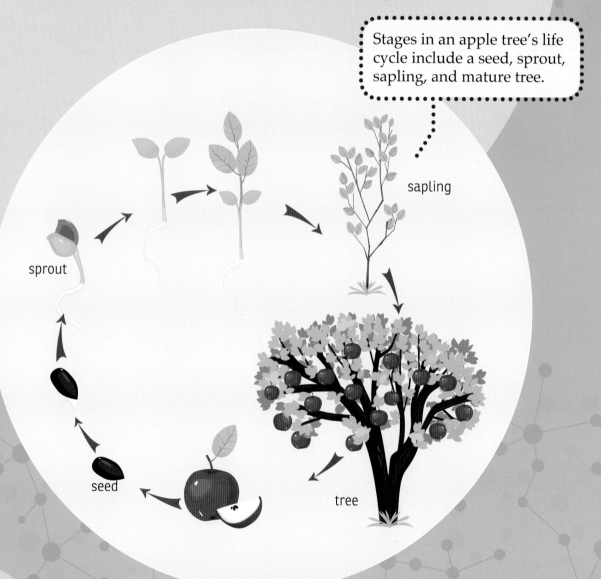

sapling

sprout

seed

tree

The Steps of Mitosis

As a plant grows, cells do not grow bigger. Rather, the cells divide to form more cells in a process called mitosis. This type of cell division begins in the nucleus. First, the DNA makes a perfect copy of itself. Then the original DNA and the copy move to opposite sides of the cell. Next, the organelles copy themselves. These copies also move to opposite ends of the cell. Finally, the cell membrane starts to pinch the cell in two. The parent cell divides into two identical daughter cells. Mitosis allows plants to grow.

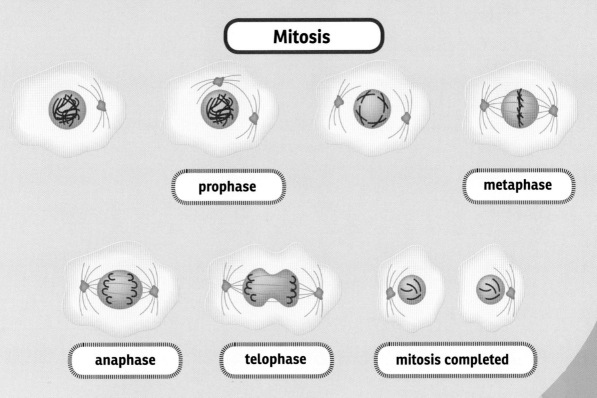

Mitosis

prophase

metaphase

anaphase

telophase

mitosis completed

Plant Growth and Seasons

In many places, mitosis is most active in spring and summer, when plants grow and produce seeds. In autumn, cell activity slows down. During winter months many plants lie dormant, or inactive. In tropical and subtropical areas, however, plants grow throughout the year. With plenty of light and moisture, plant cells can reproduce at a steady rate.

Plants become dormant during colder times of the year and when there is less sunlight.

27

CHAPTER 7

Plant Cell Types

Like all living things, plants begin as a single cell. This cell quickly divides. The first groups of cells are like blank slates. They do not have jobs yet. As cells continue to divide, they form groups with specific jobs. Those groups of cells create different plant **tissues**. Plants have three main kinds of tissues: dermal tissue, vascular tissue, and ground tissue.

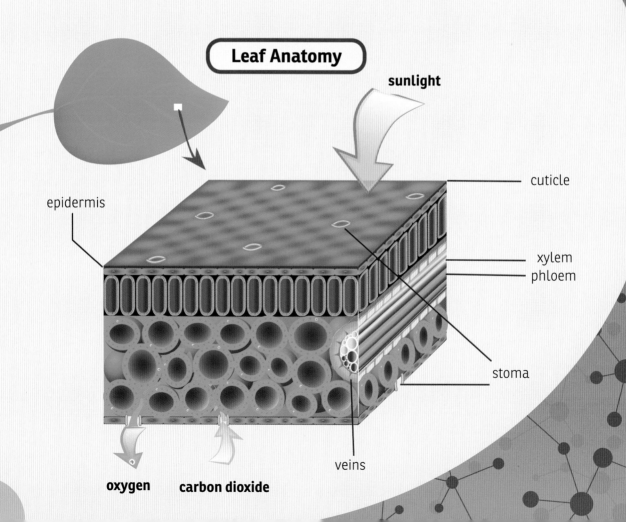

Leaf Anatomy

sunlight

epidermis

cuticle

xylem

phloem

stoma

veins

oxygen   carbon dioxide

Dermal Tissue

Dermal tissue is like skin. It covers leaves and stems and protects plants from invaders. Dermal cells let sunlight and air into leaves through small holes, or pores. These pores also release water vapor, oxygen, and other wastes out into the air. In leaves, dermal cells have a waxy coating that helps keep the plant from drying out.

Vascular Tissue

This tissue is like the veins and arteries that carry blood in animals. There are two main types of vascular cells, xylem and phloem. Xylem cells move water and nutrients. Roots take in water and nutrients from the soil. Xylem cells carry these supplies up from the roots to the rest of the plant. Phloem cells move food. They carry food from leaves down stems and throughout the plant.

Ground Tissue

Ground tissue cells fill the spaces between dermal cells and vascular cells. They make up the bulk of the plant. Most ground cells are packed with chloroplasts for photosynthesis. These green cells do the work of making food for the plant. They also have large central vacuoles for storing food and nutrients. When these central vacuoles are full of water, they help stiffen the plant so it stays upright.

tissue—a layer or bunch of soft material that makes up body parts

Glossary

acetyl group (ACETYL GROOP)—a group of acetic acid

by-product (BYE-prah-duhkt)—something that is left over after you make or do something

cellular respiration (SEL-yuh-lur res-pur-RAY-shuhn)—process used by cells to break down food molecules into small units of energy

cellulose (SEL-yuh-lohs)—material that helps make cell walls stiff and rigid

convert (kuhn-VURT)—to turn something into something else

gene (JEEN)—tiny unit of a cell that determines the characteristics that an offspring gets from his or her parents

organelle (or-guh-NELL)—a small structure in a cell that performs a specific function and is surrounded by its own membrane

oxidation (AHK-suh-day-shuhn)—the act or process of combining with oxygen

photosynthesis (foh-toh-SIN-thuh-siss)—the process by which plants make food using sunlight, carbon dioxide, and water

pollen (POL-uhn)—a powder made by flowers containing sperm produced by a plant's male organs

ribosome (RIH-bo-sohm)—structure that helps put together proteins

tissue (TISH-yoo)—a layer or bunch of soft material that makes up body parts

trait (TRATE)—a quality or characteristic that makes one person or animal different from another

wilt (WILT)—to droop

Read More

Duke, Shirley. *Cells*. The Science of Life. Minneapolis: ABDO Publishing Company, 2014.

Garbe, Suzanne. *Living Earth: Exploring Life on Earth with Science Projects*. Discover Earth Science. North Mankato, Minn.: Capstone Press, 2016.

Spilsbury, Richard and Louise. *Cells*. Essential Life Science. Chicago: Heinemann Library, 2014.

Internet Sites

FactHound offers a safe, fun way to find Internet sites related to this book. All of the sites on FactHound have been researched by our staff.

Here's all you do:

Visit *www.facthound.com*

Type in this code: 9781515772583

Check out projects, games and lots more at
www.capstonekids.com

Critical Thinking Questions

- What are the two processes of cell division in plants?

- Explain the processes of photosynthesis and cellular respiration.

- A plant cell has two borders: cell membrane and cell wall. Define each term.

Index